Fact Finders™

Energy at Work

# Solar Power

by Josepha Sherman

**Consultant:**
Steve Brick, Associate Director
Energy Center of Wisconsin
Madison, Wisconsin

Capstone
press
Mankato, Minnesota

Fact Finders is published by Capstone Press
151 Good Counsel Drive, P.O. Box 669, Mankato, Minnesota 56002
www.capstonepress.com

*Library of Congress Cataloging-in-Publication Data*
Sherman, Josepha.
    Solar power / by Josepha Sherman.
    p. cm.—(Fact finders. Energy at work)
    Summary: Introduces the history, uses, production, advantages and disadvantages, and
future of solar energy as a power resource.
    Includes bibliographical references and index.
    ISBN 0-7368-2474-X (hardcover)
    1. Solar cells—Juvenile literature. 2. Solar energy—Juvenile literature. [1. Solar energy.]
I. Title. II. Series.
TK2960.S46 2004
333.792'3—dc22                                                           2003015053

**Editorial Credits**
Gillia Olson, editor; Juliette Peters, designer; Alta Schaffer, photo researcher; Eric Kudalis,
    product planning editor

**Photo Credits**
Cover: Solar photovoltaic panels in the Mojave Desert outside Bakersfield, California,
    Corbis/Roger Ressmeyer

Bell Labs, Lucent Technologies, 13
Corbis/Joseph Sohm/ChromoSohm Inc., 10–11; Royalty Free, 1, 8, 9, 18–19; Underwood &
    Underwood, 14
Getty Images/AFP/Robyn Beck, 4–5; Hulton/Archive, 12
NASA, 7, 15
NREL/John Lenz, 17; Robb Williamson, 23; Sandia National Laboratories, 21; Warren
    Gretz, 24, 25
Stellar Sun/William Ball, 27
TRIP/Fiona Good, 16

apple
8-2-04
16.95.

# Table of Contents

Chapter 1 Solar Fuel. . . . . . . . . . . . . . . . . . . 4

Chapter 2 The Power of the Sun . . . . . . . . . . . . . 6

Chapter 3 Solar Power History . . . . . . . . . . . . . 10

Chapter 4 Capturing Light. . . . . . . . . . . . . . . 18

Chapter 5 Benefits and Drawbacks . . . . . . . . . . . 22

Chapter 6 The Future . . . . . . . . . . . . . . . . . . 26


Fast Facts . . . . . . . . . . . . . . . . . . . . . . . . 28

Hands On: Solar Sandwich. . . . . . . . . . . . . . . 29

Glossary . . . . . . . . . . . . . . . . . . . . . . . . . 30

Internet Sites. . . . . . . . . . . . . . . . . . . . . . 31

Read More . . . . . . . . . . . . . . . . . . . . . . . 31

Index . . . . . . . . . . . . . . . . . . . . . . . . . . 32

# Chapter 1

# Solar Fuel

Every two years, a group of funny-looking cars makes a 2,300-mile (3,700-kilometer) trip using no gasoline. The cars are powered by shiny black squares covering the car bodies. These cells turn sunlight into electricity to power the car. The cars race in the American Solar Challenge. This race runs from Chicago, Illinois, to Claremont, California.

The cars can only use a solar-powered **battery** system. These cars weigh less than one-third of a normal car. Top cars average 40 miles (64 kilometers) per hour along the trip.

The 2003 winner of the American Solar Challenge was the car built by a group from the University of Missouri–Rolla.

Colleges, companies, and clubs from around the world compete in the race. Many of them want to improve solar technology. They also bring attention to the possibilities of solar power.

# Chapter 2

# The Power of the Sun

Solar energy comes from the Sun. The Sun gets its energy from **nuclear fusion**. All things, including the Sun, are made up of elements. An **atom** is an element in its smallest form. Atoms have a center, called a **nucleus**. In fusion, the nuclei of two atoms join.

The Sun gives off great energy during fusion. The energy reaches Earth as sunlight and heat. Plants, animals, and people need the Sun's light and heat to survive.

The Sun is a hot star that gets its energy from tiny atoms joining together.

## The Beginning of Most Energy

Almost all energy starts as solar energy. Plants need sunlight to grow. When plants die, they rot. The soil presses down on them. After millions of years, plants turn into **fossil fuels** like oil and coal. We use fossil fuels to create electricity and to run cars and trucks.

Plants need sunlight to grow.

The Sun also drives the water cycle. The water cycle makes hydroelectric power possible. The Sun's heat makes water evaporate into a gas in the air. This water vapor soon changes back into water and falls as rain or snow. The water refills rivers and oceans. Hydroelectric power is made from the moving water of rivers and oceans.

Solar energy also makes wind. The Sun heats some pockets of air. When warm air hits cooler air, wind is created. People can use machines to turn wind energy into electricity.

▲ Water that runs through dams is constantly renewed by the water cycle, which is driven by the Sun.

## FACT!

The temperature on the Sun is 10,000 degrees Fahrenheit (5,500 degrees Celsius). Nuclear fusion creates this high heat.

# Chapter 3

# Solar Power History

For thousands of years, people have used direct solar energy. Ancient people built their houses to face the Sun. In winter, their baked clay homes took in and stored the Sun's heat.

## Experiments with Solar Power

In 1767, Swiss scientist Horace de Saussure built the first solar oven. He made several sizes of black-lined boxes with glass tops. He put the boxes inside one another and set them in the sunlight.

The ancient Anasazi of the southwestern United States built their homes to use solar energy.

Horace de Saussure built the first solar oven in 1767.

The temperature inside the smallest box rose above the boiling point of water. People later used this idea to create solar water heaters.

## Photovoltaic Effect

In 1839, Edmund Becquerel found out that some materials produced electricity when put in sunlight. He discovered the **photovoltaic effect**. Photo means light. Voltaic refers to electricity.

Scientists had little use for this discovery until the mid-1900s. In 1954, Bell Laboratories made the first solar cell out of silicon. Silicon is a pure form of sand. The silicon was better than most materials at making electricity.

In 1954, Bell Laboratories used their newly-invented silicon solar cells in one of the first solar panels.

## Uses for Solar Power

In the late 1950s, the U.S. space program needed a power source for **satellites**. In space, satellites receive direct sunlight. Batteries could store energy for times when a satellite was in Earth's shadow. Solar cells were expensive. But a dependable power source mattered more. The *Vanguard I* satellite was launched in 1958. It was the first satellite powered by solar cells.

The *Vanguard I* used electricity from solar cells to send information to Earth.

Janice Brown
flew the
*Gossamer
Penguin*, the
first piloted
solar airplane,
in 1980.

Except for the space program, solar technology was not widely used for many years. The cells were too expensive. In the 1970s, the price of oil went up. People wanted different energy sources. Scientists explored the uses of solar power.

Solar cells were used in many ways. Engineers designed solar-powered cars and boats. In 1980, Janice Brown flew the first piloted solar-powered airplane.

## Solar Power Today

The price of solar cells has come down. For most people, solar cells cost more than other ways to get energy. Some people far from other energy sources find solar cells to be cheaper than running power lines.

Peru's Uros people use solar power for electricity. They live on floating reed islands on Lake Titicaca where power lines do not run.

▲ Scientists in remote areas can use solar power to run computers.

Most solar cells are used in small items like watches and calculators. Lawn mowers and computers can be solar powered. Some people use solar-powered machines when they are away from other power sources.

To use solar power at home, people usually put solar panels on the roof. Solar-powered homes usually draw extra power from electric power plants.

# Chapter 4

# Capturing Light

Today, people use both small and large solar projects. They use solar water heaters. They build their homes to use the Sun's heat. Large solar power plants have been built to use solar energy.

## Today's Solar Cells

Solar cells look like pieces of dark glass. They come in several sizes. When sunlight shines on them, an electric current is made.

Many cells laid together make a panel. A panel may supply part of a home's energy needs. Many panels together make an **array**.

Mirrors reflect light onto water-filled rods. The water gets hot and is used to make electricity at this concentrator solar power plant.

## Solar Power Plants

Not many solar power plants exist, but two basic kinds can be found. The first type uses solar cells to make sunlight directly into electricity. The second type uses mirrors to concentrate light that heats a liquid.

The tower is one type of **concentrator** system. Flat mirrors reflect light at a tower. The tower is filled with a liquid.

Tower concentrators use sunlight to heat water, oil, or liquid sodium in a central tower. ▼

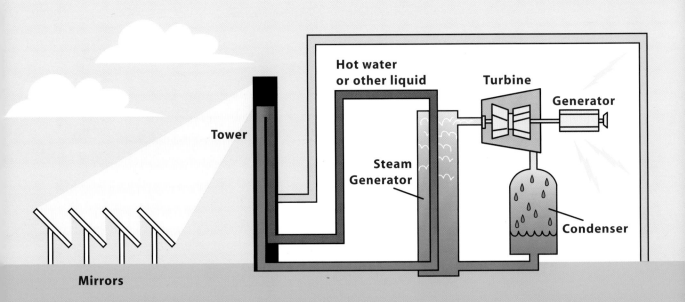

Hot water or other liquid · Turbine · Generator · Tower · Steam Generator · Condenser · Mirrors

Sunlight heats the liquid to a high temperature. The liquid is then piped through tanks of water. The water boils to create steam. The steam turns fan-shaped turbines that are connected to a generator. The generator makes electricity.

▲ Solar I near Barstow, California, was the first solar concentrator power plant in the United States.

# FACT!

Many arrays have motors to allow them to rotate toward the Sun as it moves across the sky. This rotation allows the most sunlight to be used at all times.

# Chapter 5

# Benefits and Drawbacks

Today, solar energy makes up less than 1 percent of the energy used in the United States. The drawbacks of this power source reduce its popularity. Still, solar power has many benefits.

## Benefits

Solar power is a clean, plentiful source of energy. It produces no pollution. Enough sunlight comes to Earth in one day to supply the planet's energy needs for a year. Solar energy is most available during the day, when power is most used.

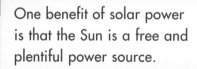

One benefit of solar power is that the Sun is a free and plentiful power source.

Solar power is a renewable resource. The Sun will shine for billions of years. Earth will probably run out of oil, coal, and natural gas in a few hundred years.

## Drawbacks

Solar energy is not available at night. It is greatly reduced on cloudy days. To be used all day, solar energy made during sunny times must be stored. Some energy is lost when transferred to batteries.

Solar power systems sometimes use many batteries.

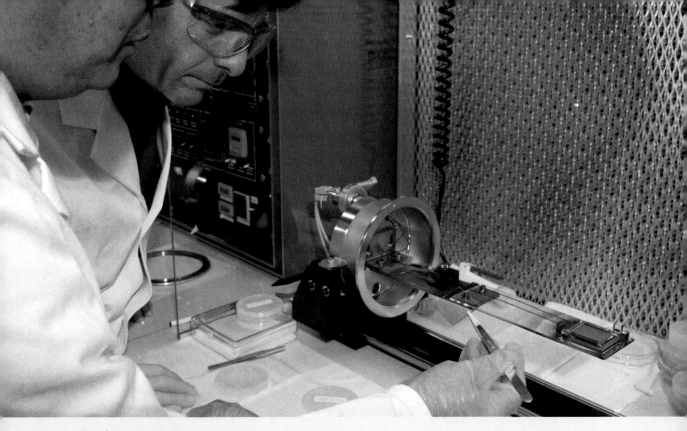

▲ These scientists
work to make
more efficient
solar cells.

Solar cells are expensive and
inefficient. Solar cells do not turn most of
the sunlight that hits them into electricity.

Scientists continue to build better
solar cells. The first solar cells turned
only 6 percent of the light that hit them
into electricity. Today, new cells can turn
20 percent of the sunlight that hits them
into electricity.

# The Future

Making better solar cells will certainly help the future of solar power. But the future of solar energy will also depend on finding more ways to use solar cells.

Companies now make new types of solar cells. They can make windows, roof shingles, and other materials from solar cells. In the future, solar cells may be in more everyday items.

People are likely to see more use of solar power in the future. Other fuels will eventually run out. Since the Sun is such a plentiful power source, people will continue to find ways to use it.

A man lays solar-cell shingles on his roof.

# Fast Facts

- The Sun produces energy through fusion.

- Most energy starts as solar energy, including the energy from fossil fuels, hydroelectric power, and wind power.

- In 1839, Edmund Becquerel discovered that some materials produce electricity when hit by sunlight. He discovered the photovoltaic effect.

- Bell Laboratories made the first silicon solar cell in 1954.

- Solar energy is a renewable resource.

- Solar energy is clean and plentiful, but solar power equipment is costly.

- In the future, people hope to make solar cells that can turn more sunlight into electricity to bring the costs down.

# Hands On: Solar Sandwich

You can build your own solar-powered oven. Be careful! The oven can get as hot as your kitchen's oven. Have an adult help you with this activity.

**What You Need**
cardboard box large enough to hold a cheese sandwich
aluminum foil, enough to completely line the box
piece of glass large enough to cover the open box top
two slices of bread and a slice of cheese
a spatula

**What You Do**
1. Line the inside of the box with the aluminum foil. Make sure the inside is completely covered with foil.
2. Put the sandwich in the center of the box.
3. Put the glass lid on the open top of the box.
4. Place the solar oven in direct sunlight.
5. When the cheese melts at the edges of the bread, the sandwich is ready to eat. Have an adult help you remove the glass. Carefully use the spatula to get the sandwich out without touching the oven.

# Glossary

**array** (uh-RAY)—a large group of solar panels

**atom** (AT-uhm)—an element in its smallest form

**battery** (BAT-uh-ree)—an electric storage device

**concentrator** (KON-sin-trate-uhr)—a type of solar power plant where mirrors reflect light on a liquid-filled object in order to heat the liquid, which is then processed to make energy

**fossil fuels** (FOSS-uhl FYOO-uhls)—coal, oil, and natural gas, formed from the remains of ancient plants and animals

**nuclear fusion** (NYOO-klee-uhr FYOO-shuhn)—the joining of two nuclei, which creates energy

**nucleus** (NYOO-klee-uhss)—the core of an atom

**photovoltaic effect** (foh-toh-vohl-TAY-ik i-FECT)—the ability of some materials to produce electricity when exposed to sunlight

**satellite** (SAT-uh-lite)—a spacecraft that is sent into orbit around Earth; satellites often take signals from one place on Earth and send them to another place.

# Internet Sites

FactHound offers a safe, fun way to find Internet sites related to this book. All of the sites on FactHound have been researched by our staff.

Here's how:

1. Visit *www.facthound.com*
2. Type in this special code **073682474X** for age-appropriate sites. Or enter a search word related to this book for a more general search.
3. Click on the **Fetch It** button.

FactHound will fetch the best sites for you!

# Read More

**Graham, Ian.** *Solar Power.* Energy Forever? Austin, Texas: Raintree Steck-Vaughn, 1999.

**Jones, Susan.** *Solar Power of the Future: New Ways of Turning Sunlight into Energy.* Library of Future Energy. New York: Rosen Publishing Group, 2003.

**Snedden, Robert.** *Energy Alternatives.* Essential Energy. Chicago: Heinemann Library, 2002.

**Vogt, Gregory.** *The Sun.* The Galaxy. Mankato, Minn.: Bridgestone Books, 2000.

# Index

American Solar Challenge, 4–5

array, 18, 21

battery, 4, 14, 24
Becquerel, Edmund, 12
Bell Laboratories, 12, 13
benefits, 22, 23, 24
Brown, Janice, 15

cars, solar, 4, 5, 15
concentrator system, 19, 20–21
cost, 14, 15, 16, 25

drawbacks, 24–25

electricity, 4, 8, 9, 12, 16, 18, 19, 20, 21, 25

fossil fuels, 8, 15, 24
fusion, 6, 9

hydroelectric power, 9

panel, 13, 17, 18
photovoltaic effect, 12
pollution, 22
power plants, 17, 18, 19, 20–21

satellites, 14
Saussure, Horace de, 10, 12
silicon, 12, 13
solar cells, 14, 15, 16, 18, 20, 25
    invention of, 12, 13
    products made with, 4–5, 14, 15, 17, 18, 26, 27
solar oven, 10, 12
Sun, 6, 7, 10, 23, 24, 26
    and other energy sources, 8–9

water cycle, 9